Thanks to Tim
25/4 1991

Olle

TIBET

Kevin Kling

TIBET

with 96 illustrations, 91 in color

THAMES AND HUDSON

ACKNOWLEDGMENTS

I would like to express my thanks to the following for
their help and for having allowed me to accompany the
Franco-Chinese geological expeditions to Tibet:

Li Ting Dong, Xiao Xu Chang, Han Tonglin (Ministry of
Geology, Peking), Claude Allegre (Institute of Global
Physics, Paris), Guy Aubert (National Institute of
Astronomy and Geophysics, Paris), François Proust,
Maurice Mattauer, Jacques Mercier, Rolando Armijo, the
Vice-Governor of the Autonomous Region of Tibet, Rolf
Winter and Andreas Catomas (Geo Magazine) and Béatrice
Allavène.   K.K.

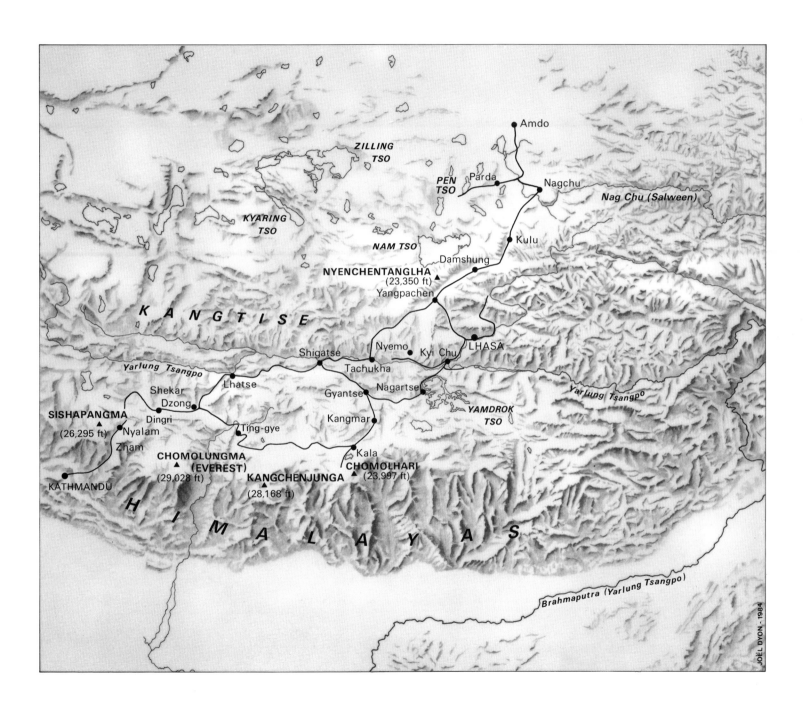

ZILLING TSO

PEN TSO

Parda

Nagchu

Nag Chu (Salween)

Amdo

KYARING TSO

NAM TSO

Kulu

Damshung

NYENCHENTANGLHA
(23,350 ft) ▲

Yangpachen

K A N G T I S E

Nyemo

Kyi Chu

LHASA

Shigatse

Tachukha

Yarlung Tsangpo

Lhatse

Gyantse

Nagartse

Yarlung Tsangpo

Shekar Dzong

Kangmar

YAMDROK TSO

SISHAPANGMA
(26,295 ft) ▲

Dingri

Nyalam

Ting-gye

Kala

Zham

CHOMOLUNGMA
(EVEREST)
(29,028 ft) ▲

CHOMOLHARI
(23,997 ft) ▲

KATHMANDU

KANGCHENJUNGA
(28,168 ft) ▲

H I M A L A Y A S

Brahmaputra (Yarlung Tsangpo)

JOËL DYON - 1984

For Paul

Introduction

In recent years, it has been possible for travellers to reach the high valleys of the Afghan Pamir, the Karakoram, Ladakh and Nepal with little difficulty. Yet, it has been several decades since any Westerner has been able to cross the formidable mountain belt – and political barrier – of the Himalayas to penetrate into the *real* Tibet. Among the last to do so were Sven Hedin at the beginning of this century, Alexandra David-Neel between 1914 and 1924, and Giuseppe Tucci and Heinrich Harrer in the thirties and forties. This was an impenetrable country, even in the days when the political situation was less of an obstacle. As Harrer recounts, a visa had to be sought from the local *dzongpön*, or high official, in order to stay in his town, while obtaining permission to visit Lhasa, the 'Forbidden City', was particularly difficult.

Tibet's geographical boundaries added to the problems, with the Kunlun and Altyn Tagh ranges to the north, the Himalayas to the south, the Pamirs to the west and the high mountains of Szechwan to the east. Roads were bad, and the only means of travel in the interior were on foot or by horse or yak. Until recently, there was no wheeled transport, and the story is told of how the King of Nepal, on a visit to Tibet, had to have his car completely dismantled and carried piece by piece across the Himalayas by Sherpas.

As a result, Tibet remains today, for Westerners, one of the last great unexplored regions on earth. Most of the country is a vast plateau at an average height of some 15,000 feet above sea level (Mont Blanc, the highest peak in the Alps, reaches 15,781 feet). In the rolling hills and steppes, immense lakes give birth to many of Asia's mightiest rivers. For example, the Tsangpo cuts through the Himalayas to become the sacred Brahmaputra in India, and the Nag Chu ('Black River') becomes the Salween as it flows through Burma and along the border of Thailand. The Mekong, the Yangtze and the Hwang Ho rush down hundreds of miles of precipitous gorges to irrigate the rice fields of China and Indo-China that feed more than a quarter of mankind.

In 1980, the People's Republic of China timidly reopened the borders of what now forms one of its largest provinces to a limited number of foreign tourists and mountaineers, most of whom have only been permitted to pay brief visits to Lhasa, the capital, and to Shigatse. In that same year, however, I had the privilege of accompanying two French geological expeditions, which gave me the opportunity of reaching the remotest places, travelling thousands of miles by road and track across the roof of the world: north as far as Amdo, in the heart of the high plateau, as well as the length and breadth of the valleys that skirt the Himalayas between Lhasa and Kathmandu. Apart from Lhasa and Shigatse, our lodgings in this harsh and unpredictable climate were in Chinese military camps or small Sino-Tibetan agricultural communes.

Lhasa: Place of the Gods

Lhasa, the administrative and religious capital of Tibet, has been bustling with activity since August 1980, when a radical change in Chinese policy allowed the reintroduction of some freedom of worship and a certain amount of private commercial activity for the first time since the Chinese takeover in 1950. Today, pilgrims throng from all parts of the country to visit the oldest and holiest temple, the Jokhang. Built in AD 650, this place of worship was dedicated by the great king Songtsen Gampo to his two wives (one Chinese and one Nepalese) as proof of his adherence to Buddhism, the faith that he himself had introduced to replace the animistic Bön beliefs as the official religion of Tibet. An original mural painting still survives inside the temple, depicting the famous monarch and his wives, their images now somewhat blurred by a sooty deposit from the lamps that are kept alight with molten yak-butter.

On a visit to the Jokhang, I was able to watch hundreds of fervent worshippers as they queued up, with infinite patience, to enter each little chapel in turn and to receive the blessing of the resident lama. All kinds of gifts were offered to the gods and demons, with some of the faithful placing pins in a piece of sacred cloth. Nobody failed to kiss the golden feet of the precious Shakyamuni, the imposing statue of the Buddha that dominates the centre of the sanctuary. A lama showed me up a steep, narrow ladder, beautifully constructed and worn smooth by countless thousands of feet, that led to the gilded rooftops and lavishly decorated beams. A constant tinkling sounded from the multitude of bells attached to the eaves as a protection against evil spirits. It was from up here that one could enjoy the best view over Lhasa, dominated by the mountains and the Potala in the background and with the crowded streets and alleys of the city below.

Outside, a dense crowd was circling in an endless clockwise movement around the temple, ceaselessly muttering the sacred mantra *Om mani padme hum*. The most devout Buddhists prostrate themselves in the dirt as they chant the holy words. There was a time, it is said, when pilgrims would come from as far away as Mongolia, performing *kyangchak* all the way. This is a religious exercise that consists of stretching out on the ground with the arms above the head, marking the point that the hands reach, and then starting again from that mark.

Lhasa is divided into two quite distinct sections. The entire modern part surrounding the Potala palace has been built by the Chinese during the past thirty years. It is in these new block-shaped buildings with corrugated-metal roofs that the majority of the Han population lives. The Potala itself was mostly built by the 'Great Fifth' Dalai Lama, Ngawang Lobsang Gyatso, in the seventeenth century, and has been the residence of all successive Dalai Lamas up to the present fourteenth holder of the title, who fled to India in 1959.

In the sixteenth century, Sönam Gyatso, third Abbot of the Reformed Church (the Gelugpa or Yellow Hat sect) of Tibet, was the first to be known as 'Dalai'. The title was conferred on him as a gesture of thanks by the Mongolian prince Altan Khan, whose spiritual mentor he had been. The term 'Dalai' is simply the Mongolian equivalent of the Tibetan honorific 'Gyatso' ('Ocean') borne by all Tibetan rulers, and the title Dalai Lama thus carries the meaning 'Ocean of Wisdom'. Although this is the form known to China and the West, in Tibet the Dalai Lama is referred to as Gyalwa Rinpoche or 'Precious Conqueror'.

Other aspects of the new section of Lhasa helped to give it a typically Chinese look. Most of the people, dressed uniformly in

Wall painting in the Norbulingka palace, Lhasa

greens or blues and wearing Mao-style caps, rode bicycles on the newly paved streets. A Chinese girl proudly showed off her 'modern' sewing machine on the pavement outside the general store, which was stocked mainly with Chinese goods. However, specifically Tibetan tastes were also catered for in the form of aprons, brightly flowered scarves and yak-skin or felt boots with upturned toes.

The other part of Lhasa, the old part, is completely Tibetan. At the entrance to the old town, people set up tents, together with their sheep and yaks and the rest of their modest possessions. Frequently, they sell or exchange goods or ornaments, either in the open market or in the rows of small shops that encircle the Jokhang. Here can be found cloth, skins, turquoise and coral jewellery, and silver bowls for *tsampa* (the national dish of roasted barley flour which is mixed with butter and tea) among a host of other items. At the time of my visit to the old quarter, some new buildings were being constructed in a neo-Tibetan style with brightly painted window shutters, and the streets were being repaved in stone. The market had been temporarily moved to Barkhor Street, the sacred way that surrounds the Jokhang, making the ceaseless procession of pilgrims all the more colourful. It was June, and fruit and vegetables were in short supply, but the autumn harvests would bring apples, cabbages and radishes to the daily market, where they would be sold alongside the inevitable mounds of rancid yak-butter heaped directly on the bare pavements.

Another commodity commonly on sale is fresh yak-meat, which may be displayed in slabs neatly draped over the branch of a tree or else piled on the wheelbarrow that has brought it straight from the slaughterhouse. I discovered this place, which is simply an open courtyard, after visiting the mosque. The proximity of the two is, in fact, no coincidence, since the task of killing the animals falls mainly to the Moslems. As Buddhists, Tibetans view butchery with abhorrence, since it entails the taking of life, and the butcher's trade (which is hereditary) is regarded as one of the lowest in the social scale, along with that of blacksmith and disposer of the dead. Curiously enough, and in spite of this, the slaughtering-yard was not the only place where a yak might end its days. Several times I witnessed the killing, skinning and cutting up of an animal on the open pavement in the centre of the city – a sight which seemed to go unnoticed by other passers-by. Only a few small children looked on with a sense of dumb bewilderment.

Land of the Highest Lakes

The road north from Lhasa goes directly to Peking, more than 2,500 miles and three weeks' hard travelling away. For more than six hundred miles, it crosses the inhospitable wilderness of the high plateau before reaching the more populated areas of western Qinghai and Gansu. Setting out along this road, we followed the course of the Yangpachen river as it snaked through a gorge lined with pink-striped sandstone and purple volcanic rock. Suddenly, we seemed to cross a distinct line where the poplars and willows disappeared. We were now above 13,000 feet.

Our first stop was Yangpachen, not a real Tibetan village, but a Chinese military settlement situated beside some hot springs, where water boils just below the earth's surface. The Chinese have built a geothermal plant to convert this enormous natural power source into electricity, and tall pylons already carry high-voltage cables a large part of the way towards Lhasa. One day, the capital, which already makes use of solar heating, will rely on these hot springs for the vast bulk of its energy needs.

It was near Yangpachen that I was invited for the first time into a Tibetan home, a whitewashed, single-storey mud construction with only one room. Here I shared with my hosts some Tibetan-style tea – a smoky, topaz-coloured beverage made with rancid yak-butter – and ate *tsampa*, which sticks to the palate like peanut-butter but is naturally nourishing and seems ideally suited to keep out the cold. Clouds of asphyxiating smoke from the yak-dung fire billowed to every corner of the house, whose walls were bare except for a solitary poster of Mao Tse-tung. The room quickly filled up with village neighbours, curious to see the stranger. Wrinkled women of indeterminate age wore patched and torn skin *chubas* (long-sleeved, loose Tibetan cloaks), which, like the men, they draped in traditional fashion below the right shoulder, so that that sleeve hung down loosely by the side. They sat close together by the single window, through which a diagonal shaft of sunlight strove to illuminate the dark, smoke-filled interior.

Exploring the region on horseback can be a nerve-racking experience, since the horses in Tibet insist on walking along the very edge of the track, which often overhangs dangerous precipices. This is a result of the fact that almost every animal has been accustomed to carrying a load, and in order to prevent this from banging up against the cliff face, it has acquired the habit of keeping right to the outside of the path. On one occasion, my stocky Mongolian pony and I shared an unexpected experience. A dozen or so huge Himalayan griffon vultures were eagerly feasting on what appeared to have been a *kyang*. Disturbed, the birds, heavy from overeating, hobbled lazily away, while a couple of them took off and swooped low over our heads. Only the bones of the unfortunate *kyang* were left. *Kyangs* are a kind of wild horse (in fact, the ancestor of the donkey) which are extremely shy and elusive and move with the graceful gait of a deer. They are approximately the same size as a horse, although their heads are larger in proportion to their bodies. Their coat is light brown and their belly white, which makes them appear more graceful and slim-looking. They are creatures of the wide open spaces and perish in captivity, being unable to endure the loss of their freedom and refusing to take food gathered by human hands.

Vultures feed not only on the carcasses of animals, but on human corpses as well. In fact, this so-called 'heaven' or 'air' method of disposal, the most common in Tibet, is used in the case of all ordinary persons who have died a natural death, including lamas of the lesser ranks. In order to induce the vultures to eat, it is necessary for the body to be dismembered, which is done by making cuts in a swastika pattern, starting at the shoulder blades. (In Tibet, the swastika, called the *yung-drung*, is a symbol of good luck.) There are three other forms of funeral rite: by water, fire or earth. Water burial is held in the least esteem and is generally reserved for lepers, criminals and beggars, whereas cremation is only for great lamas and high officials. When the body is completely burned, the bones, which break easily in the hand like charcoal, are taken to the lamasery and mixed with mud. From this compound are moulded several thousand miniature *tsa-tsas* (terracotta figures or bas-reliefs), which are preserved in a large

whitewashed *chörten* built of mud and stone outside the lamasery. The temporary *chörten* in which the body was cremated is destroyed. Earth burial is reserved only for those who have died from some highly infectious disease or for the very highest (incarnate) lamas, such as the Dalai and Panchen Lamas. The bodies of such holy men are embalmed and placed in the bases of huge gilded copper *chörtens*, decorated with precious stones. The finest examples of these are the mausoleums of the Dalai and Panchen Lamas in Lhasa and Shigatse. *Chörtens*, which have their origin in the ancient stupas of India, are religious monuments consisting of five levels which represent the five elements: earth, water, fire, air and space.

Once I came across a row of five dilapidated *chörtens* in the open country, not far from Yangpachen. Hiking up the mountain to examine them more closely, I could see that two of them had been more severely damaged than the others, presumably by the Red Guards. Tibetans had since gathered up the broken stones engraved with Buddhas and carefully lined them up at the base of the monuments. There were even newly hung prayer-flags fluttering in the wind. In the same region, I saw two ruined monasteries or *gönpas* (Tibetan for 'secluded spot') in the wild landscape. The lamas who built them seem to have had a wonderful aesthetic sense, always choosing the most picturesque site, usually high up, so as to have a grand panoramic view of the surrounding valley. One of the ruins particularly impressed me, because the only thing left standing intact was an enormous prayer-wall composed entirely of engraved stones bearing the mystic formula *Om mani padme hum*.

A day's excursion in the direction of Nyemo led us into a wide valley, where we were entirely dependent on aerial photographs to guide us, since there were no roads here at all. We drove through streams (one so deep that it reached the windows of the jeep and flooded the floor), through gorges and across ravines as we forged our way over the mountainous terrain. That evening, I watched two boys and a man halt their small yak caravan for the night. It was fascinating to witness the ritual. First of all, the yaks were tied together on a long black rope, which was held to the ground with heavy boulders. After each beast was securely tied, the rugged old man and his two helpers, chanting all the time, began to unload the beautifully woven black-and-brown-striped

Wall painting in the Jokhang temple, Lhasa

yak-hair bags that they carried. Once everything was unloaded, the animals were released one by one from the rope and wandered off, not too far, to graze. When our Chinese chauffeur approached a seemingly docile yak to give it a friendly pat, one of the boys signalled anxiously to him to keep out of range of its vicious horns.

The yak is a hefty, primitive-looking beast, somewhat resembling the ancient paintings of bisons in the caves of Lascaux. The high plateau of Tibet is the natural ecological niche for this unique animal, which flourishes best at heights above about 13,000 feet. Below this altitude, there is a similar, though less powerful animal, the *dzo*, which is actually a crossbreed between a yak and a cow. Strong enough to do heavy field tasks, yaks can also seem quite playful, as even the largest of them romp and scamper about like calves. Their milk, butter, meat, dung and hair provide the basic essentials of Tibetan life. Most yaks are still wild, however, roaming by the hundred through the lonely steppes.

After the old man's yaks were put to graze, I watched how he set about lighting a fire to make tea. The elder of the two boys went around the area picking up dung and dropping it into the woven basket he carried on his back. The man then took some of the drier pieces, with which he made a pile, as one would with kindling. A silver-decorated flint and tinder pouch, with a sharp curved base, hung from the man's belt. He struck the flint a few times and then placed it inside the pile of dung, which soon began to smoke. To help the fire along, he made use of some primitive bellows made of a skin bag with a long tube attached. This he inserted inside the pile, cunningly twisting the top of the soft skin sack in such a way as to blow air through the tube, until the fire gradually took hold. The value of yak-dung in the woodless regions of Central Asia cannot be overestimated. It is the main fuel of the country and burns with a hot, steady flame.

The day arrived for our journey, still northwards, to Nam Tso, better known as Tengri Nor, the second largest lake in Tibet, the largest being Koko Nor in the northeast, near the border with China. Leaving Damshung, we followed a track which is the main route for hundreds of caravans carrying cheese, wool and salt (from the lakes) down to the south in exchange for barley and tea, the staples of Tibetan food. There are a number of caravan stops along the way, where yaks are unloaded and unsaddled and left to graze for a while. At night, being not completely domesticated, the yaks are tied up again in a circle around the tents.

It was on this track that I stopped at a place where two brown tents stood side by side in the wilderness. A young girl skilfully used her sling to gather up a herd of young yaks, which she then tied down securely. Inside one of the tents, two women, mother and daughter, were busy making yogurt and cheese. A huge vat of simmering yak-milk was placed over a fire in the middle of the tent. There was no furniture here, just some striped yak-hair blankets piled around the sides for use as beds. A lazy Lhasa apso (the Tibetan breed of terrier) watched attentively as the older woman poured some milk from the vat into a tall, narrow container to churn it. Another, thicker portion of the liquid went into a thin skin bag and was left to drip into a small bucket outside the tent. Some chunks of cheese already lay drying on a towel in the sun. A handy commodity, the cheese remains 'fresh' for two to three years, although it becomes so hard that the unwary could risk breaking their teeth on it. To Tibetan children, this cheese is as popular as sweets are in the West, and it is common to see them with lumps in their cheeks, for one piece of it can be sucked for hours. I only ever saw one other variety of cheese, in the south near Tachukha. This is made from goat's milk, which, when semi-dry, is squeezed through the fingers into twists and then left to bake in the sun.

As we were about to leave, a long yak caravan was making its way over a flimsy bridge. The leading yak was enormous and was distinguished, as is the custom, by a scarlet cloth on its black side. The others were unladen, which allowed their magnificent wooden saddles to be seen. Two noble-looking horsemen, carrying slings, headed the caravan, followed by the most beautifully dressed woman that I had yet set eyes on in Tibet. Later, I discovered that her brilliantly coloured, striped skin coat and felt 'bowler' hat were common dress amongst the women of the northern steppes of the high plateau. It is striking how similar the costumes, instruments (the sling) and the ways of life are between the herdsmen and shepherds of the Tibetan plateau and those of the Altiplano, ten thousand miles away in the Andes of South America. This probably results from their common ancestral origin in the steppes of Mongolia and from the fact that they share the same high-altitude, pastoral environment. The two

Wall painting in the Jokhang temple, Lhasa

men were brothers, and the woman doubtless their wife. Polyandry, which is common in Tibet, is a custom that became established in order to keep property or possessions (such as herds of yaks or sheep) in one family. Should the husband have one or more younger brothers, the girl must marry each of them in turn, at intervals of about a year after the first ceremony. Children of such unions look upon the eldest brother as their father, the younger being called 'uncles'.

We continued on the caravan trail by jeep, the road sometimes plunging steeply down into ravines, then rising again to over 16,000 feet, at which point it began to snow. It was from a pass at 17,700 feet that a flash of turquoise-blue appeared on the horizon. Sandwiched between banks of clouds that billowed over mountain reliefs with the outlines of ruined buildings, it appeared as sharply set off against the ochre-coloured background as the surface of a polished gem in its gold setting. The radiance of the blue was so intense that it seemed as though illuminated from within. This was Tengri Nor, 'Lake of the Heavens'. Colours are of great importance to Tibetan meditation, and blue represents infinity and permanence. Up close, the waters of Tengri Nor seemed even more peaceful than silence. Nothing moved. Not a trace was there of human or animal life anywhere in those flat amber-tinted prairies all around; just the purity and solitude of nature.

Near the lake was a village, where we were invited for a meal of tea and *tsampa*. On the wall, once again, was a poster of Mao, this time accompanied by portraits of some of his German and Russian comrades, such as Marx, Engels, Lenin and Stalin. On another wall was an old map of the world, marked in Tibetan. Such maps are now extremely rare and practically impossible to find. The continents had unfamiliar shapes, and pinned to the map was a plastic bird somewhere around what would be South America.

In these parts of the high plateau, the average altitude is about 15,500 feet. As the last high peaks gradually disappear, the landscape flattens out into rolling hills interspersed with numerous lakes. Only tent-dwelling herdsmen live here, tending their sheep and yaks, while caravans roam the wide expanses of the steppe. Nagchu is the last settlement before reaching this vast stretch of wild and desolate country. Unlike the towns to the south, many of the buildings in Nagchu are constructed with red bricks. At the time of our visit at the end of September, there was a lively atmosphere in the town, since a week-long fair was just beginning. Nomads from the various provinces of Tibet, Ü, Tsang, Amdo and Kham, had gathered to sell or exchange their wares. Coloured tents and stands lined the main street, which was decorated with Chinese lanterns. A photographer had come all the way from Peking to record the event. Curious crowds wandered up and down the street examining the goods, which, except for the greater abundance and variety of animal skins, were not very different from what was available in Lhasa. I passed a stand in the morning which offered dental care, while in the afternoon it had switched to watch repair. The men in their 'cowboy' hats, who paraded around or stopped to chat on horseback, had an air of the old Wild West. The women were dressed in the northern style that I had encountered on the caravan trail, with vividly coloured, striped skin coats reaching almost to the ground. Most people wore the traditional boots with upturned toes (*shap-cha* or *lham*), although here the designs were more fanciful and the colours brighter. Others wore Chinese-made rubber and canvas ankle-high gym shoes.

The last days of September brought the first snows of winter, falling regularly in the early mornings. Geological fieldwork would become impossible, but before retreating to the warmer and lower southern regions, we made a last reconnaissance to the west, towards the interior of the plateau. As dawn revealed a virginal white landscape, a group of wild yaks, blacker than ever against the snow, strayed across our path. It was only when the jeep got quite close that they stopped in the middle of the track to stare at the unfamiliar sight. Then, suddenly, they began to leap in all directions and galloped off, snorting and swishing their tails. Except for an occasional horseman, we were to see no other human in this desolate no-man's-land.

We crossed the Salween river and entered lush prairie-land where snow was melting in the morning sun, and finally we came to the most remote point that we were to go. On the great lake of Pen Tso, strong westerly winds whipped up huge waves. Flocks of red ducks and grey geese flew low over the water. In spite of the altitude, it seemed as though we were on the shore of some northern sea. It was just before a storm, and sombre clouds formed a gloomy veil over the surrounding jagged mountain peaks. The light was threatening and beautiful, and the landscape more like a dream than reality. However, the cold, drizzling sleet which soon began to lash our faces like a thousand fine needles was real enough. In spite of the weather, there was much excitement among the geologists, who had found the fault trace of a giant earthquake that had shaken the region thirty years earlier. The whole Tibetan plateau and the Himalayas are constantly subjected to such massive movements of the earth's crust, which have gradually given them their form. In fact, the entire plateau, with its vast mountain ranges, has been pushed up as a result of the collision of India with the continent of Asia. Earthquakes are today's evidence of this continuing process.

In the Shadow of the Himalayas

The south of Tibet contrasts dramatically with the solitary steppes of the high plateau. No more flat meadows, broad lakes or daily snowfalls; no more nomads or wild yaks. The average elevation here is around 13,000 feet, and the land is therefore more habitable. The south is thus a more densely populated and sedentary region, where people build houses and villages and cultivate the land. It is no surprise that most of the big cities and monasteries are located here.

There are high mountains (the Himalayas) and deep open valleys created by glaciers during the Ice Age. Great rivers have left irrigable terraces. The largest of all the valleys, that of the Tsangpo, extends for more than a thousand miles from west to east, just north of the Himalayan range and parallel to it. This valley lies along a deep scar in the earth's crust, marking the place where the Tethyan Ocean, which once separated India from Asia, closed some fifty million years ago, knitting the two continents together. Remnants of the dark-green rocks which once made up the floor of that ocean, more than 16,000 feet below sea level, can be found today 13,000 feet high amidst the rich lands of the Shigatse plain. Barley, wheat, fruit and nut trees, and radishes grow there, as well as some new green vegetables and cabbages that the Chinese have introduced.

It is only in July and August that the monsoon rains manage to pass over the Himalayas. Apart from this short rainy season, the climate is extremely dry. Tibet lies only a few degrees north of the Tropic of Cancer, and the sun is therefore very strong, giving the Tibetans deeply tanned skins. Many of them rub yak-butter on the skin as a protection against sunburn and dryness. By the end of October, rivers such as the Salween or Brahmaputra have dwindled from swollen, muddy torrents into tame little streams once more, after the return of the dry weather. The mud and sand which are left behind are blown by westerly winds into the valleys, giving many landscapes of the south the appearance of deserts, covered as they are with huge *barkans* (crescent-shaped dunes). Finer particles of this mud and sand are blown right across China as far east as Peking. After the dust settles, it forms a highly fertile loess deposit.

In Shigatse, the capital of Tsang province and Tibet's second city, the imposing ruins of an ancient hill-top fort dominate the surroundings. The town itself lies beneath its walls and is an important centre of trade. At the edge of the town is the famous Tashilhunpo monastery, which still stands almost intact. This is the former seat of the Panchen (Tashi) Lama, the second most important religious authority after the Dalai Lama. Two of the chapels have been reopened for worship. However, like the Potala and the Drepung monastery (near Lhasa), it is now kept mainly as a museum; only a few old monks still reside there, carrying out restoration work on the painted beams and courtyard murals and performing other general maintenance tasks. As on the roofs of the Potala and Jokhang, gilded *chörtens* decorate the tops of the central pyramid-shaped buildings, which are painted a reddish earth colour. Worshippers form a ritual procession, always clockwise, around the monastery, clambering up and down the mountainside to encircle it, while *latses* (piles of rocks and prayer-flags made as offerings to the gods or *lhas*) line the narrow path.

1st October in Shigatse, a national holiday in China to celebrate the birth of the People's Republic, was merely an occasion for the Tibetans to wear their best clothes and to relax, enjoy a picnic or play dice under the yellowing poplars near the Panchen Lama's now dilapidated summer palace. An old lama washed his beet-red robe in a stream, and it was even warm enough for a group of boys to swim in a circular pool.

Wall painting in the Jokhang temple, Lhasa

The beginning of October in the Tsangpo (Brahmaputra) valley brought idyllic rural scenes reminiscent of the paintings of Courbet and Millet. Near Shigatse, the air vibrated with songs that had the beauty of Gregorian chants as the Tibetans went about their work. I watched men, women and children cheerfully gathering in the great harvest of golden barley and wheat, even young children doing their share of reaping with the sharp, curved sickles. Once I saw an entire field of wheat cut down by hand in an hour, and by the second hour it was all bundled into stacks. Graceful rhythmic movements accompanied the tying of each sheaf. I watched carefully as a young girl picked up a handful of wheat stalks, deftly divided it into two, and then, waving her arms out and in as she twisted the ends together, braided them like a rope. Sometimes she spat on the wheat to make it twist more easily. In the late afternoon, the harvesters sat down in a circle to chatter and sip tea before finishing the day's work.

The grain was threshed in the most primitive way. The whole village took part, chasing yaks round and round the threshing floor with much shouting and cracking of whips, forcing them to trample the ears. A more usual method is to beat the grain with wooden flails. After the threshing is finished, several methods are employed to winnow and sift the grain. Normally, it is done with a long rake or pitchfork, with which the straw is repeatedly tossed up into the wind to be blown away. Next, a large, round sieve is used to sift the grain over and over again. On a windless day, I saw an ingenious system whereby four women separated the grain and the straw by flapping a sheet to create an artificial draft. The lighter straw and chaff were blown to the side, while the heavier grain formed a neat mound below.

The unexpectedly early arrival of winter interrupted the late summer with an abrupt snowfall, which covered the freshly ploughed fields and still unstored crops around Shigatse. The road to Dingri had changed greatly since the spring. The green turf where sheep grazed had turned into muddy fields, splashed here and there with white. The mossy tufts that grew beside the streams near the 17,000-foot pass had also disappeared under a blanket of snow. Our jeep struggled to make headway through a threatening blizzard. Once we reached the other side of the pass, however, the going was easier and the snowstorm much less violent. It was here that we came across the strange sight of a man casually bathing in a hot spring, oblivious of the fact that the temperature was at freezing-point outside. Washing his hair with mud, he took his time to relax as steam formed clouds around him. By the time we reached our sleeping quarters in Shekar Dzong (14,400 feet), another blizzard was raging. Snow and mist hid the citadel and the ruined *gönpa* which crowns the mountain rim. The year's crop of barley and wheat, piled in tidy heaps ready to be threshed, now lay under a covering of snow at the entrance to the town, which is built into the hill on several levels.

A Chinese military checkpoint signalled the proximity of the border with Nepal as we drove towards the Dingri valley. The morning sky had never been so intensely blue, and here snow lay only on the high peaks, with just a last vestige of it accentuating the edge of a crescent-shaped *barkan*. As we rounded a bend on the approach to Dingri, the first thrilling sight of the high Himalayan range came into view. Mount Everest (29,028 feet) stood out distinctly, its peak instantly recognizable. As Lama Anagarika Govinda said: 'There are mountains which are just mountains and there are mountains with personality.' Chomolungma (the local name for Everest) is certainly in the second category, its northern face having the hypnotic, mysterious air of a sphinx. It is impossible to avoid the magic of its spell. The Tibetans also call Everest Gang-tön Ting Gyalmo, 'Queen of the High Blue Snowy Mountain', or Mitong Gutong Chapur Long-nga, 'Mountain Visible from All Directions, on the Summit of Which the Flying Birds Become Blind'. It was an extraordinary sensation to realize that we were among the first Westerners for many years to look on the north side of the greatest mountain range in the world. Just to the west of Everest is Pumori and, beyond it, a more massive, rounded mountain, Cho Oyu, which rises to 26,750 feet. Immediately to the east of Everest is Makalu (27,790 feet), the fourth highest mountain on earth. Words cannot describe the overwhelming grandeur of this immense, harmonious landscape.

A horse drank from a deep-violet pond, while a few *dzos* grazed the ochre-coloured grass amidst the ancient, weathered ruins that were scattered throughout the valley. Nobody seemed to know whether these were evidence of a long-forgotten Mongol invasion or due to some natural disaster. Perhaps they were *tasams* (caravanserais) or the walls of *gönpas*. No one could say. A solitary puff of white cloud floated in the azure sky above one of the ruins. In Tibetan Buddhism, the cloud symbol is of great importance. Present in most *thangkas* (scrolls) and temple paintings, the cloud represents the creative power of the mind, which can assume any imaginable form. The white cloud especially (or even a cloud in the pastel colours of the rainbow) is regarded as the ideal creative medium for the enlightened mind.

Between Dingri and Kung Tso, a group of Tibetan shepherds appeared as though from nowhere. One of them, who was spinning wool wrapped around one arm, gave the friendly and respectful Tibetan sign of greeting by sticking out his tongue. Two were playing guitar-like instruments and dancing Tibetan jigs, laughing all the while. Following them, we came to an unusual public bath-house. A mud-brick construction stood on a hill where many little streams bubbled up from within the rock. From one particularly deep crack, a constant flow of hot water poured into a natural pool, around which a lama had built a house. He lived here and ran the spa with two elderly ladies. Outside the house was a *latse*, or pile of prayer-rocks, with the usual engraved *mani* stones. From here, I watched as other shepherds left their sheep and horses down in the valley and climbed the hill for their

bath. Before going in, one of the men stopped to 'wash' his hair with earth. First he unbraided his long black tresses, then, bending over, vigorously rubbed the dry mud through each lock. Next, he washed the hair with a bar of brown soap, and finally rinsed it several times in one of the hot springs. Inside the building, a steaming pool was surrounded by a number of small rooms or cabins, in which people could change, rest or have tea after their bath. A cow stood near the shadow of the door, while the high peaks, and Mount Everest itself, could be seen from the pool, beyond the open roof of the bath-house.

On our way back to Lhasa, we took the southern route which runs parallel to the base of the Himalayas. Beyond the mountains lie Sikkim and Bhutan. Soon the landscape became infinitely more inhospitable and huge *barkans* of sand spread out on every side, their monstrous curved shapes sometimes reflected in a lake. Near Kala, howling October winds chased the clouds above the jade-green waters of Ram Tso beneath the Chomolhari range, announcing winter. The majestic Kula Gangri peak floated on a blazing coral sunset. The moon was a silvery-white, wafer-thin crescent suspended in the mist. The time had come to leave the 'Throne of the Gods' for the real world below.

Wall painting in the Norbulingka (summer palace of the Dalai Lama), Lhasa

Captions

1 Gaurisankar (23,440 feet) rises abruptly above the steppes of the Tibetan plateau, where thousands of sheep find pasture.

2 A lone horse in the Kung Tso valley.

3 Turquoise-blue is not only the colour of Tibetan jewels (north of Nyonni Ri, 22,143 feet).

4 On the high plateau of Tibet, most yaks are still wild, wandering in their hundreds over the steppe (near Zilling Tso).

5 Nomad camp beside Ram Tso at the foot of Chomolhari.

6 Tibetan women braid their hair with brilliantly coloured silk threads.

7 A Tibetan woman washes her hair in a hot spring at Tsangmuda, near Chomolungma (Mount Everest).

8 A rare view of the north side of the Himalayas. Everest (29,028 feet) is in the centre, with Makalu (27,790 feet) on its left and Pumori and Cho Oyu (26,750 feet) on the right. They tower over the ruins of Buddhist *gönpas* and ancient caravanserais in the Kung Tso valley, itself some 15,000 feet above sea level.

9 Tashilhunpo, the great monastery of Shigatse, was built in 1447. It was, until recently, the seat of the Panchen (or Tashi) Lama, second after the Dalai Lama in Tibet's religious hierarchy.

10 Pilgrims in an alley of the Tashilhunpo monastery, Shigatse. Like most large monasteries in Tibet, Tashilhunpo was a complete city, sheltering at times thousands of lamas and pilgrims.

11 A young lama (a rare sight now in Tibet) in the Barkhor procession around the Jokhang temple, Lhasa.

12 A lama inside the Tashilhunpo monastery, Shigatse.

13 A pilgrim on the monumental steps of the Potala palace, Lhasa.

14 The Potala palace in Lhasa was built in the seventeenth century under Ngawang Lobsang Gyatso, the 'Great Fifth' Dalai Lama. The Dalai Lamas lived in the central red buildings, the top floor of which contained the principal apartments of the present (fourteenth) bearer of the title.

15 The kitchen of the monastic 'city' of Drepung. Once teeming with life, most monasteries are now deserted or populated by only a handful of ageing lamas.

16 A lama at his window in the Tashilhunpo monastery, Shigatse.

17 Harvest in the Yangpachen valley.

18 Southern Tibet is a land of contrasts: sand dunes lie next to fields of newly harvested barley.

19 Each carrying a sickle, Tibetan women go out to the harvest near Nyemo.

20 Mountain barley ripens at the end of the rainy season, in late August. Roasted, ground and mixed with butter and tea, it becomes *tsampa*, the staple foodstuff of the region.

21 Simple wooden rakes are used to winnow the grain.

22 Many women find it practical to wear trousers instead of the more traditional Tibetan dress for harvest work.

23 Autumn colours on the shores of Kala Tso.

24 Sifting barley near Ting-gye.

25 Threshing floor in the Tsangpo valley.

26 Sifting grain near Tachukha.

27 A mid-afternoon break for butter-tea.

28, 29, 30 When there is no wind, a large blanket is used to create the draught needed to separate the chaff from the grain, as here at Nyemo.

31 Kula Gangri (24,780 feet) towers above the Kala steppe, itself almost 15,000 feet above sea level.

32 Dust storm on the Kyi Chu river.

33 A young girl with traditional turquoise-and-coral earrings and necklace.

34 In another two weeks, at the end of the monsoon rains, the barley will be ripe for harvest.

35 Abandoned *gönpa* in an isolated village.

36 In Central Asia, the Tibetan plateau is known as the 'land of storms'.

37 Even in summer, it does not rain above 15,000 feet in Tibet. All precipitation comes in the form of snow and hail, which rapidly whiten the landscape and the green leaves of the trees (near Liu Chu).

38 Heating milk to make yoghurt and cheese (near Damshung). Some Tibetan cheese becomes so hard and dry that it can be kept for three years and has to be chewed for hours before it can be swallowed.

39 The white walls of this traditional Tibetan house in Shekar Dzong are lined with cakes of dried yak-dung, for use as winter fuel.

40 A lama restores the paintwork on the wooden beams of an inner courtyard of the Tashilhunpo monastery, Shigatse.

41 Tibetan children flying kites from the roofs of Shigatse.

42 The dry air and burning tropical sun redden the cheeks (in the Norbulingka, the Dalai Lama's summer palace in Lhasa).

43 Mother and children in the Sera monastery.

44 Children on the threshing floor near Tachukha in the Tsangpo valley.

45 Children playing during the harvest, near Tachukha.

46 A young man in Gyantse.

47 Pink sandstone in the Yangpachen valley.

48 Late October in the Tsangpo valley. As a dust storm in the distance announces winter, hefty yaks work the fields with primitive wooden ploughs.

49 Autumn landscape near the Kyi Chu river. The region near Lhasa is not as high as most other areas of Tibet, which enables willows to grow here.

50 A yak caravan passing some ancient ruins in the Kung Tso valley. Caravans carry cheese, wool and salt from the high pastures and lakes in the north to the rich valleys in the south in exchange for barley and tea.

51 A wool caravan in the high steppe, near Nagchu.

52 A caravan makes a stop near Kulu. The yaks are tied in a circle for the night, surrounding the nomads' tent.

53 For both men and women, horses provide the principal means of travel over the vast plateau (near Damshung).

54 A night halt near Tengri Nor.

55 A traditional sign of welcome: a young shepherdess sticks out her tongue (near Kulu).

56 The shores of Yamdrok Tso twist in and out of ancient valleys like the arms of a fjord.

57 Similarities of altitude and way of life, probably combined with a common ethnic origin somewhere in northeastern Asia, have produced a remarkable resemblance between the Tibetans and the Indians of the Bolivian Altiplano.

58 Because the Tibetan plateau is ringed by mountains, many rivers cannot escape the highlands and end in large lakes, such as Pen Tso (15,400 feet).

59 On the shores of Pen Tso.

60 Tengri Nor (Nam Tso or 'Lake of the Heavens'), the second largest lake in Tibet, lies at the foot of the Nyenchentanglha range.

61 Tibetan horsemen are closely related to the fierce Mongols who, led by Genghis Khan, dominated thirteenth-century Asia (near Yangpachen).

62 Shepherdesses in the steppe, near Parda.

63 An evening hailstorm breaks over the jagged peaks of the Chomolhari range and the jade-green waters of Ram Tso, just south of Kala.

64 Pen Tso, and the other great lakes of Tibet, are the summer refuge of many rare migratory birds.

65 Waves break on the sandy shores of Pen Tso, in the heart of the high plateau.

66 Tibetan horsemen gather at the September fair in Nagchu.

67 At the Nagchu fair.

68 Yak-meat, much appreciated by Tibetans, is sold in the streets. Lhasa apsos wait patiently for the leftovers.

69 A family shares a meal of *tsampa* and butter-tea in the back streets of Lhasa.

70 Behind a mother and her child in Barkhor Street (the sacred way around the Jokhang in Lhasa), a woman sells juniper for ritual offerings.

71 Mounds of rancid yak-butter are preserved in yak-skins and displayed on the pavement for sale.

72 An old woman carries her grandchild to market.

73 The free market on Barkhor Street in Lhasa. Smoke fills the air as juniper burns in great copper cauldrons, and fresh vegetables provide a welcome alternative to the Tibetans' monotonous diet of *tsampa*.

74 Inside the Tsangmuda bath-house, a lama enjoys a hot bath. The water temperature from the natural hot springs is 40°C (104°F).

75 A Tibetan family in Nagchu.

76 A Chinese tug-boat powers the ferry across the Tsangpo near Tachukha.

77 A young Tibetan girl in Nyemo.

78 The ancient wall and octagonal *chörten* of the Palkhor temple in Gyantse.

79 Children use the irrigation reservoir at Shigatse as a swimming pool.

80 Salt flats in the Pum Chu valley of the northern Himalayas. The brilliant white salt is produced by numerous mineral springs which flow into the rivers.

81 In winter, fine dust and sand are blown by westerly winds to form huge crescent-shaped dunes or *barkans*.

82 Yak caravans near the end of their long southbound journey, beneath the peaks of Everest and Makalu.

83 A caravan crossing a moraine.

84 Great skill is needed to ride yaks, which detest being mounted.

85 The bridge in Shekar Dzong.

86 Early October snow blankets the newly harvested barley crop in Shekar Dzong.

87 Inside the flour-mill in Tachukha. The miller pours the grain into a woven funnel placed above the centre-hole of the granite millstone.

88 The millers break off for a meal of *tsampa* and butter-tea in Tachukha.

89 Women repairing the irrigation canal near Shekar Dzong.

90 An early winter snowfall brings an end to summer in Lhatse.

91 A white cloud, with its constantly changing form, symbolizes for Tibetans the creative power of the mind.

2

3

4

5

6

9

12

13

18

17

20

21

22

24

28

29

30

37

39

40

4

42

46

47

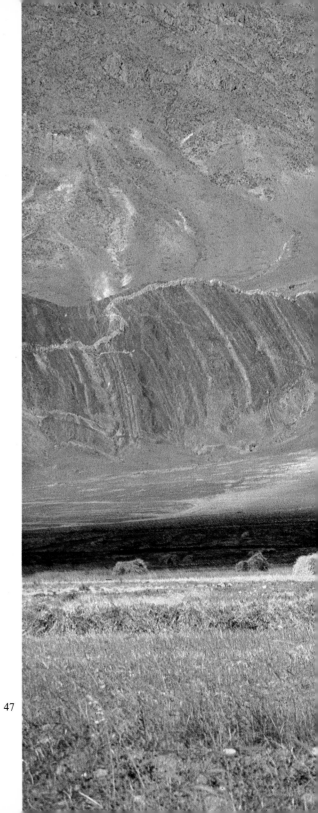

58   59

64

65

70

71

84

89